Job

Readiness

with Brittany Phelps-Jones

The Keys to Getting the Job

&

Keeping the Job

Table of Contents

My Experience

Hi, I'm Brittany, and I will be accompanying you throughout your journey to *getting the job* and *keeping the job*.

To start, I'm not going to lie to you as if I have always gotten the job, or even kept the job for that matter. What I will tell you is that I've had my share of both sides.

I started from the bottom of a company and worked myself up the ladder to the point where I set my own prices now instead of accepting what's being offered for the position. I have witnessed everyday situations from the perspective of an employer as well as an employee. It's not easy but both can be rewarding in the end.

Let's get into the next chapter two.

Why Are You Here?

Take a moment and a few deep breaths.

Now, ask yourself, *"Why am I here?"*

Do you want to go to work every day just to earn a paycheck?

Do you want a career or profession?

Why are you here?

You may think this is a silly question, but the why will have a lot to do with if you get the job **and** keep the job. If you're going to work every day just to earn a paycheck, then chances are you will struggle with both getting the job and keeping it. Until you are 99.9% sure of your why, you won't be motivated to obtain or maintain any positions being offered.

Think about this: the version of you interviewing for a fast-food restaurant vs. the version of you interviewing for a managerial position with a well-known company.

I know that the presentation should be the same for both scenarios. Did you? Now I'm not saying break out the suit and tie, but business casual is a thing - no bonnets, flip flops or pajamas allowed. Which brings us to section three.

Getting the Job:

From the Application to the Interview

Now that you understand your why, drum roll please!!! Let's talk about getting the job - from the application to the interview.

First things first, now that you know the why, the **where** shouldn't be hard; and by that, I mean selecting the location of job you need/want to work shouldn't be hard.

Here are the next steps to take.

⇒ Research positions and companies of interest. Use your notepad to make an organized list, listing them in the order of highest to lowest interest.

⇒ Familiarize yourself with their brand and mission; again – this may be significant information to document in your notepad.

⇒ Be fluently able to discuss how your addition can be an asset to the company. *Your resume should reflect these same qualities. Your resume should be a written billboard of your experiences, your accomplishments and your achievements. Your resume is normally your first impression, and we all know that the first impression may be the last impression depending on how well it went.*

Next let's talk about the application portion of getting the job. On the application you want to –

⇒ Be honest and thorough with information being provided.

⇒ Always attach a detailed resume highlighting the experience you report on the application. *If unfamiliar with terms in application, don't be afraid to familiarize yourself with terms before continuing. This means taking out the time to google or ask for help.*

⇒ Always complete the application in its entirety.

Finally!!! It's time to interview. Always, and I do mean always, prepare to interview as if it's your first day of work. Grooming is one of the most important aspects of interviewing. If you don't look the part, it may not be given to you.

Remember to

> ⇒ always dress neat and clean.
>
> ⇒ be free of body odor.
>
> ⇒ brush your teeth.
>
> ⇒ wash your face.
>
> ⇒ comb your hair.
>
> ⇒ dress for success.

You must always have the mindset that the position is already yours.

Also, remember to answer interview questions thoroughly and specifically.

If you don't understand the question, ask the interviewer to rephrase the question or elaborate more about what they are looking for. Sit up straight, smile and be honest concerning their expectations as well as yours. Never settle for anything because they won't settle at all.

Job Readiness

Congratulations you're over halfway through the course, and ready to get to work. Let's talk about some basic factors centered around successfully maintaining a job. Once in any position with any company you want to learn your position and be the best at it. Once you've achieved this you want to cross train for other positions in the company as well when time permits and with approval from your supervisor. This paired with other qualities create what we call job security. Let's talk about those other qualities for a moment. Being prompt and on time, properly dressed for position per dress code, must be well groomed and must have a friendly yet professional demeanor to both internal as well as external customers. Look at it like this, how great would your customer service scores be if you treated each interaction with each person as if you were assisting a potential employer. I bet your customer service scores would skyrocket right along with the sales. Remember we don't just want to get the job we want to keep the job.

The Price of Admission

This is the price paid for entry. How does this relate to job readiness you ask? When you take on a new role or position with any company, the same way they are agreeing to pay you for doing the job you are agreeing to do the job without accommodation. You have to be willing to follow policy and procedures. Which is another reason why you should do your homework prior to entering into the agreement. This way you will have time in advance to determine if it's a good fit for you and vice versa. You must have the ability to change as policies tend to change from time to time. Make sure you come to work daily and on time ready to work. Bring your motivation and be ready to learn new things that offer job security. There are those words again, you'll see it often throughout your journey to keeping the job.

Keeping the Job

Yaay!!! You are here, you have officially and successfully created a resume, applied for a job, interviewed, been hired and are steadily working towards keeping the job. You did it!!! Don't stop there, this is where the hard work really begins. Remember that phrase job security? Well tag, you're it!!! This is the period you go through relentlessly training and bettering yourself, making yourself more of an asset to a company. Now you're able to get additional hours filling in for other positions. Not only that but you're also being looked at for alternate roles with your company, because of your hard work, training, professional demeanor and how well you carry yourself. You are now qualified for better. Remember you deserve this, no one can determine your outcome but you!

The Assessment

The assessment is a scored test that is given during the application process. This test tells potential employers what type of employee you might be. News Flash!!! They don't want to know you personally. They want to know the "you" that is a potential employee/representative of their company. They want to know how reliable or how trustworthy you would be.

Lastly.. remember...

The Interview

During the interview process while you're '*wowing*' your potential employer with your experiences on your resume be sure to make eye contact to let them know you're paying attention.

Sit up straight and speak proper English when responding to the interviewer.

Be friendly and professional as if it was just another day on the job.

Always arrive to interview at least 15 minutes prior to actual start time.

Then *let your light shine bright.*

Sell yourself.

MAKE THEM WANT TO GIVE YOU A CHANCE.

My Job Search (Notes)

_____

_____

_____

_____

_____

_____

_____

_____

_____

_____

_____

Message From the Author

Hi again, I'm Brittany. I have over fourteen years in retail management. I have done everything from cleaning toilets to managing teams of 100. I have won customer service awards and trophies as well as in shrink and sales. I give 1000% wherever I may land. It's always been about the possibilities form me, starting in one place then ending up in another.

"*Why are you here*?" is a question I've asked myself often and whether it is managing my own company, managing someone else's company or both at the same time - my love for customer service has never changed.

During my time in retail management, I saw how so many deserving people were denied opportunities based off results of assessments or appearances alone. I just wanted to do my part in assisting someone in being better and taking their seat at the table. <u>Be worth it</u>.